I'll Root for You

You

and other poems

Written by
Edward van de Vendel

Illustrated by
Wolf Erlbruch

Translated by
David Colmer

Eerdmans Books for Young Readers

Grand Rapids, Michigan

A Magic Place

Seconds left before the start.
All your fans are shouting hard.

They're convinced that you'll do great.
Breathe in deep and concentrate.

And suddenly the racket dies.
You've gone deaf, but don't know why.

You block them out. Your thoughts turn in.
A wind gets up inside your skin.

It builds up to a hurricane
that twists and roars around your brain

and bends your body to its will.
You're tensed and ready, standing still.

The storm has seized you in its hands.
You leap. You're off. You are the champ.

And while they roar and root for you,
you're not there—and that's sports too.

You've trained your body year on year,
but only when your mind is clear

and blank—*when you're not there*—
can your body cleave the air.

It takes you to a magic place.
This is sports. You win the race.

Your greatest dreams can all come true,
but only ever without you.

The Bottommest

Everything a rhino says
has a clear, sharp, undeniable point.
Rhinos never pussyfoot around the joint.
Their statements are short but bold.
They always think extremely large.
At most they clear their throats
before they charge.

A hippopotamus
always gets to the bottommest.
Their faces are heavy with gravity.
Their thoughts don't wander.
They plunge down deep
and plow through mud
in search of things to ponder.

And you know what they do
with their heavyweight muscles?
The discus and shot put and hammer-throw shuffle.
They do judo and sumo
and any sport where you don't need to diet.
If XXL's welcome,
they're happy to try it.

There.
That's what prejudiced people say.
And maybe what they're really like
doesn't matter anyway.
But I happen to know a hippo
who only ever says things that are silly,
and a rhino who only whispers
(he's really hard to follow),
and a figure-skating elephant. *Really?*
Yes. Really.

Tree Sports

Are there trees that always worry
about who's short or bent or small?
Does a growing oak keep lists
of which oaks are getting tall?
Are there sports for beech and birch trees,
with chestnut referees?
Do elm trees have a league
where they're judged on boughs and leaves?
Does a pine tree watch the records
because there's one it hopes to break?
Are we innocent spectators
at a slo-mo willow race?
Are there tree trunk sports divisions
as to height and breadth and more?
Is a forest just a game in play?
Is somebody keeping score?
Does every nut and acorn
long to be the very best?
Does every little seedling
want a medal on its chest?

Please don't let it be so.
Let them grow without a fight.
Let them slowly live their lives
without a clue of passing time.

Because if even trees are in a rush,
what can we lean on
when we've run ourselves
into the dust?
And if even branches want to win at any cost,
in whose arms can we climb
for consolation
when we've lost?

Poem

"Listen up, now, little brother,"
says one boxer to the other,
"cuz I dunno if ya know it,
but I'm also a great poet.
So listen to my poem
about my punches, how I'll throw 'em.
I've got a jab that's just for you, nice and sharp and just for you.
I've got some hooks and they are too, fast and heavy, just for you.
That's a few to get me going.
There are more that I'll be throwing—
and then and then and then and then—
I'm the one who's won again."

That's what he says as he dances around.
Then his opponent knocks him down.

And with the poet on his back,
the other boxer says, "Know what, Jack?
That wasn't such a lousy poem,
about those punches and how to throw 'em,
but some parts were just plain wrong.
We can fix it, won't take long.
Where you said *I*, you meant *you*.
And you meant *me* when you said *you*.
Swapping them is all you need to do.
Except one bit.
That 'won' bit,
this is the fun bit.
Change that to *'then and then and then,*
I'm the one who's lost again.'
So how's it end?"

"I've lost again?"

"Exactly! That's much righter.
You're a better poet than a fighter."

Grandma, Knitting

When I was your age
(says Grandma, knitting),
the mountains were five times as wide,
and five times as steep, and wild,
and they screamed all the time,
"Look at that kid, we've got to
      get rid of her!"
and then they stood up—yes,
then the mountains stood up,
and they shook you off, *thwup*,
and there you were, upside-down.

When I was your age
(says Grandma, still knitting),
we found dragon tracks every day,
and footprints of ogres you mustn't
      disturb,
and we disturbed them.
I lost a lot of friends that way—
Felix to a yeti,
Boris to a nasty kind of goblin,
and poor old Hetty,
gone completely, except for one ear
and a little toe.
Oh dear,
things like that happen, you know.

When I was your age
(says Grandma, still knitting away),
we saw bears here and bears there.
On the way to school
I'd see ten every day.

Those bears were always eating menswear.
But that wasn't the worst.
Worse was that the owners of the menswear
had been eaten first.
Those bears would follow us down the street,
all the way to school,
and then the bears would come upstairs,
and we kids could only sit and pray
Miss Gray would give them someone else
to eat instead.
Yes, that's the kind of life we led.

Grandma, that's not true, is it? you say.
Grandma, you're just joking, right? you ask.
How could you go outside to play?
Oh, says Grandma, easy—
in pieces.
Mom cut me into three,
then my legs could go and ski,
and if they had an accident,
Mom still had two-thirds left,
and she sometimes had a spare bit too.
So she'd put me back together at night, with glue.
Anyway, your scarf's done now,
so off you run,
go have some fun out in the snow.

What do you mean,
you think you'll just stay home?

Impossible Beats Possible

Imagine that everybody playing sports
suddenly
one day
stopped on the spot.
Just when they're about to hit or serve or kick,
just when they're dodging or trying to pass.
A basketballer in mid-dribble,
a batter in mid-swing,
a tennis player dangling from her racket
with her racket dangling from the ball.
I can see the headlines now:
FROZEN IN MOTION!
WHO PRESSED PAUSE?
But then
—with a bang—
they're playing once more
and together, all at once,
against the odds, they score.
Imagine that for a moment if you can:
everyone relieved, everyone celebrating!
The greatest joy you've ever seen,
the biggest thrill.
Impossible beats possible,
two hundred million to nil.

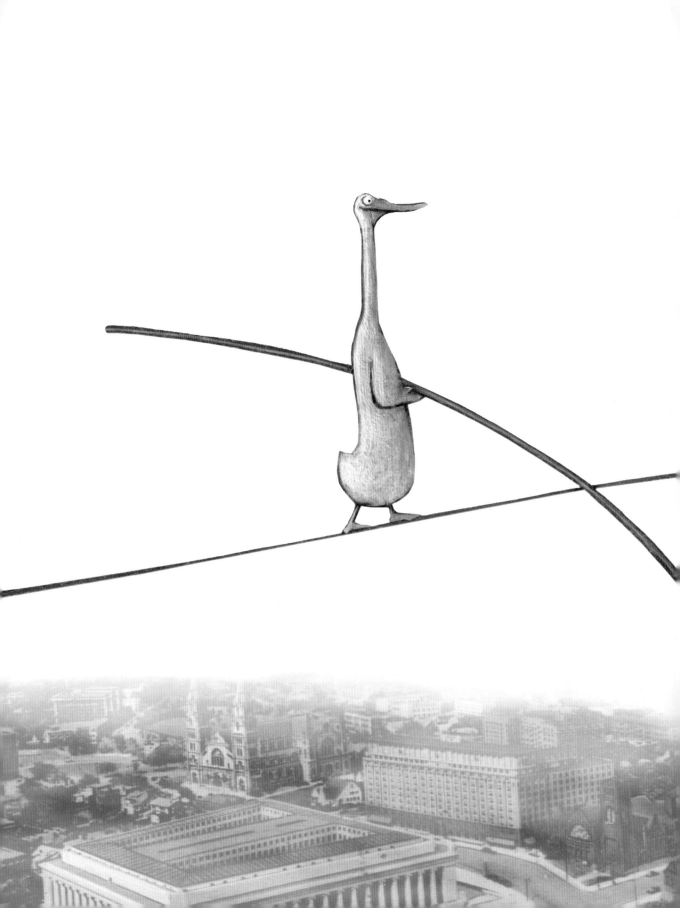

Stretch a Rope Tight

Stretch a rope tight over it.
Over
the things they said that got stuck in your head.
Over *oh, you'll learn*, over *just do what you're told*,
over *you think you're so smart*, over *just teasing*, over *shut up, will you*,
over *you're wasting your life*, over *you'll never make it*, and over
both feet on the ground, over common sense and off in the clouds,
over snickers and wisecracks behind your back,
sometimes mumbled, sometimes rude—
stretch a rope tight over it
and take the first step,
and then another,
then another,
and let everyone who wants to stay low down
look up at you.
Let them compare themselves
to who you dare to be.
You walk your own tightrope,
confident,
full of concentration,
and they stand there
looking up
with neck-ache admiration.

I'll Root for You

I root for you
because of the muscles whose speed you have tamed.
Because of the days that you patiently trained
to learn how to race and how to go slow.
Because fans call them "players," but the players are stayers,
who get bored by training and then train some more.
Because you must wait if you want to get great,
and the wait takes forever, and the great parts are short.

I root for you
when you suddenly shine,
when you leave your old self way, way behind,
bursting out of your skin to go for the win,
on the right track, at the right time,
during the right lap, in the right fight.

And afterward I'll root for you
when you can hardly believe that it's now coming true.
I'll root for you with the cheers in your ears.
For the sun that will shine with you as its heat,
for all of our hearts, with you as their beat.

But also,
if one day you can't find the storm,
the whirlwind on the inside you thought you could trust,
if you fall, if you fail,
if you're starting to fade,
if you're maybe exhausted,
if you have to decide
that this time you're beaten, and bear it with pride,
then too,
I'll root for you.
Because this is my place, and I'm here to stay,
behind every finish and on every day,
no matter where, no matter when.
Now get up, get out there,
and go win again.

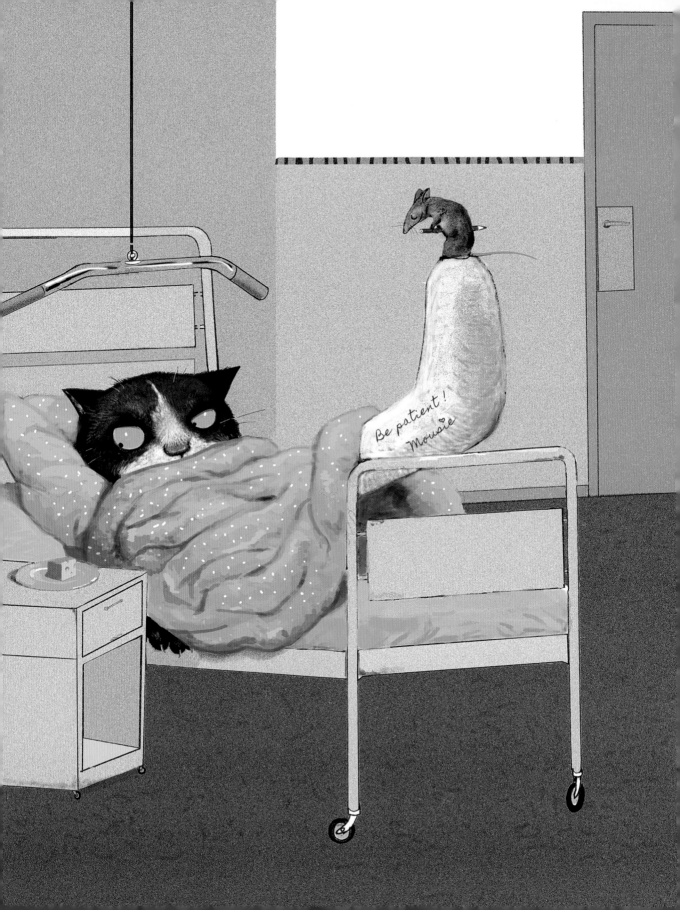

I Did Warn You

I *did* warn you.
Don't go skateboarding during the hippo spring migration.
I mentioned it in our last conversation,
through the hole in the baseboard.
You ignored me, of course.
You even called me a nag and a busybody,
and a nasty little mouse,
and then you left the house
without paw-guards or kneepads and not
even a helmet on your head.
Halfway through the tiger trot.
Halfway through the rhino ride.
Halfway through the panda pride.
And now you're stuck in bed.
And whose fault is that?
And I should have mentioned it before,
but did you want some cheddar cheese?
None left, I'm afraid.
All gone, along with the mozzarellas and the bries.
Gobbled up. Such a shame.
We couldn't control ourselves anymore.
But no one's keeping score.
No time for that
now the rodent rodeo's under way.
Oh,
did I forget to tell you?
It started yesterday.

A Message from Our Sponsor

Our water is a gift from above,
it fits like a glove!
Our water moves as you swim—dog-paddle, breaststroke, or crawl.
Just dive right on in! One size fits all!
It slips on so easy, it's silky and wet—
the best-tailored garment you've ever had yet.
Dressed in our water you'll make a big splash!
You cannot buy better with credit or cash.
A jacket of aqua, a jumpsuit of blue,
to dress best when swimming, our water's for you.
This outfit is seamless and wonderfully cool.
We'll clothe you with pleasure—
we're your local pool!

(Because they paid for this message—
it was written for them, on commission.
So tomorrow when you pay your admission,
recite this poem perfectly,
word for word,
and as part of the deal you'll get in for free!)

(Oh, and if they shake their heads
at these lines,
and say that they don't know 'em,
okay, fine,
this *wasn't* a sponsored poem.)

Ski Jumpers

In January, in Austria,
they whiz down on their skis,
Hansi & Petri & Matti & Olli,
all take off perfectly.

And oh, the wind is strong this year—
a record-breaking chance.
Hansi & Petri & Matti & Olli
don't land till they're in France.

Of course, they're on the news that night—
it's never been done before—
but Hansi & Petri & Matti & Olli
just want to fly some more.

They jump in front of every storm,
and fly from land to land.
Hansi & Petri & Matti & Olli
win thousands of new fans.

Until the springtime comes again,
and they can rest their legs,
then Hansi & Petri & Matti & Olli
go south to lay their eggs.

That's where we get ski jumpers from.
They hatch from eggs like birds.
They nest all summer in Liechtenstein,
at least that's what I've heard.

So bye, Olli & Matti & Petri & Hansi,
we love you and wish you the best.
We hope you have a fabulous vacation,
and an eggstra happy nest.

Here's the Idea

Today we'll root for the losers.
Today we'll cheer the other way round.
Today we'll love everybody
whose somersault
never got off the ground.
We'll back the bumblers,
support the stumblers,
the bunglers.
No banners today
for those who go fast.
On the winner's stand?
Last, second, and third to last.
With flowers and kisses
for all the also-rans.
The winners?
They can slink off with their heads bowed.
Today strength and speed will not wow.
Tomorrow they can be heroes again and more.
For now our champs have never won anything before
(and if they came close,
they immediately blew it).
That's our idea.
Yes, let's do it!

(So we put it to the meeting,
and everyone was moved
because none of us had ever won
anything,
nothing,
not even most-improved.)

The Mini-Hummingbird

Oh,
this is a secret
only runners
know.

You start and it goes well.
Your heart is ringing like a bell,
and the other runners all can tell
that you're the one to beat today.
Until you suddenly drop back.
Your feet are heavy on the track.
Hey!
Someone passes on your right,
another on your left.
What's wrong?
Every step you take's uphill.
You try to force it with your will,
but your will has gone downhill.
But then,
then,
the mini-hummingbird is there,
a teensy, tiny bird of air
that flies and flutters beside your head
as if it's made of gas or glass,
a sigh with whizzing wings
that whispers as it sings.

It shoots off straight ahead,
and though you don't believe a word
of this and know there's no such thing
as a runner's hummingbird,
you open the chase
and pick up the pace
and win the race.

And afterward,
a reporter asks, "Tell us,
what exactly happened there?"
and you think of what you saw in the air—
the tiny little bird you'll remember forever,
but you just say,

Oh,
that's a secret
only runners
know.

Creation Day

Warm and sleepy and inside,
you open up the curtains wide
and see that snow is falling down.
It makes you laugh and dance around,
and now your hands and feet can't wait
to grab and stamp and throw the snow,
so out into the yard you go.
It's great!
You're the king of cold,
and all this white belongs to you.
You know exactly what you want to do.
You make a ball that you can roll,
and as you roll, you watch it grow.
Today is your creation day,
and tomorrow on the news they'll say:
Little kid
makes world of snow.

Frogs Win!

Something most people don't like
one little bit
(being different from the rest)
has been a sport for millions of years,
and in that sport
frogs are clearly the best.
Oreophryne ezra, for instance, is black when it's little,
but grows up pink. And do you know what *Rhacophorus*
vampyrus can do? Fly when it jumps! It never touches ground.
Its tadpoles just float around. With vampire fangs!
There are also frogs that, when they're scared for their life,
break off a leg and use it as a knife. There are male frogs
whose noses grow when they smell a female.
There are frogs that moo and frogs that sing like birds,
there are cowboy frogs (they seem to wear spurs),
there are frogs that look through eyes like slits,
there is *Rheobatrachus silus*, which, I kid you not,
hatches eggs in its stomach and gives birth through its mouth!
Oh, and then there's the frog that's just a quarter-inch long.
In short,
in this sport
if I said frogs were doing a thousand times better than you or me,
I wouldn't be wrong.
Line up your friends and you'll see what I mean—
the same number of ears and toes,
and the same old legs
with the same old jeans,
the same old, same old.
In the Diversity Olympics,
frogs take gold.

Harry, or How a Cyclist Fell

1.

There came a day
that Harry had panted so much
he was suddenly wearing a jersey
made by panting away.
He had on panted pants too,
and a panted helmet on his head,
the kind you couldn't buy anywhere
not even for a million dollars,
because it was made of air,
exhaled and coalesced
(that means bunched up together)
in a special layer.
It was the lightest and the best.
Later, on the descent,
he was also wearing a panted jacket
with panted buttons
and a panted collar.

2.

When he got home he was still stunned,
but for a bit of fun,
he panted his wife a bracelet
and a pearl necklace,
and whatever else she liked.
"H–here," he said, "I know
you h–hate me always being on my bike,
but now—you h–have
some compensation."
And he panted her a lovely matching
h–handbag, h–hairband combination.

3.

So did Harry's puffed-up outfit
make him go faster than the rest?
No.
But the ones you can't outsprint, you can always outwit!
And though I don't like to be a taleteller,
Harry soon panted himself a propeller!
And a tailwind, and wings,
and all kinds of helpful things,
and then he was always first across the finish line.
He won a race, then won the next nine.
He was the champ in Rome and the champ in Paris.
He did so well he was almost embarrassed.
He went fast,
he went even faster,
but that only led to disaster.
Because the union realized he had to be a cheater,
and trapped him with a brand-new specially invented breath-doping meter.
Disgraced. Replaced.
And first Harry said, *No, no, no, that's not me.*
But then he confessed.
Live, on TV.

4.

Does someone like Harry have a future,
now that he's been caught?
None. Zilch. Zero. Naught.
He stays home and doesn't say a word,
and now I've heard
his wife's run off—with a h-h-h-hockey player.
Harry stares into space.
He isn't going anywhere.
Sometimes he pants himself some cotton candy,
watches it hang in the air, and then
he sucks it in again.

5.

Oh, what a sad and lonely fate.
He thought he was panting his way to heaven,
and he's ended up in hell.
But—what did you expect?
That he'd get another chance?
And maybe go on to win a Tour de France?
Or three, or four?
Or maybe even
seven?

Zis Little Piggy

"Zis little piggy comes from Holland,
and zis little piggy, he had him a dream.
He wanted to be champion on the bars,
the rings, and the beam,
but his little piggy football team
said, 'You? In a leotard?
And zen you swing down and swing up,
and everybody looks at your butt.'
'Ha-ha-ha-ha-ha-ha-ha-ha-ha,'
zey laughed so long and hard,
zey were so mean.
But people,
zey grunted a different tune,
when little piggy did his routine.
Because he won a gold metal.
His dream came one-hun-dret-per-cent true.
So let me tell you, dear childrens,
if piggy can do it, so can you.
I tell you, Never lose fate in yourself
I tell you, Maybe the world will giggle, but so what?
Zat's no biggy.
Just follow the piggy
and show zem your butt.
Let piggy be your example!
Let piggy be your man!
Oh, my little piggy babies,
you oinksolutely can!"

Edward van de Vendel has written dozens of books for children and young adults, including *The Dog That Nino Didn't Have*, *A Dog Like Sam*, and *Sam in Winter* (all Eerdmans). He was nominated for the Astrid Lindgren Memorial Award in 2011 and 2012. He lives in the Netherlands. Visit his website at www.edwardvandevendel.com.

Wolf Erlbruch is a German illustrator and children's book writer. His previous books include *Duck, Death and the Tulip* and *The King and the Sea* (both Gecko Press). He was awarded the Hans Christian Andersen Award for illustration in 2006, and in 2017 he became the first German to win the Astrid Lindgren Memorial Award.

David Colmer is an Australian writer and translator. He has translated more than sixty books throughout his career, including *A Pond Full of Ink*, *A Dog Like Sam*, and *Sam in Winter* (all Eerdmans). His translations have won several prestigious awards, such as the IMPAC Dublin Literary Award and the Independent Foreign Fiction Prize. He lives in Amsterdam.

First published in the United States in 2018 by
Eerdmans Books for Young Readers,
an imprint of Wm. B. Eerdmans Publishing Co.
2140 Oak Industrial Dr. NE, Grand Rapids, Michigan 49505
www.eerdmans.com/youngreaders

Originally published in the Netherlands in 2013 by Em. Querido's Kinderboekenuitgeverij
under the title *Ik juich voor jou*
Text © 2013 Edward van de Vendel
Illustrations © 2013 Wolf Erlbruch
The illustrations were originally published in Wolf Erlbruch's Children's Calendars © 2004, 2009, 2011, 2012, and 2013
Peter Hammer Verlag GmbH, Wuppertal.
English-language edition arranged through mundt agency, Germany
English-language translation © 2018 David Colmer

Manufactured in China

27 26 25 24 23 22 21 20 19 18   1 2 3 4 5 6 7 8 9

ISBN 978-0-8028-5501-5

A catalog record of this book is available from the Library of Congress.

Nederlands letterenfonds
dutch foundation
for literature

Publication was aided by a subsidy from the Dutch Foundation for Literature and the Mondriaan Foundation.